Level 1: 300 vocabulary words

# Nüwa, the Goddess of Mankind

## 女娲的故事

韩颖 改编

MP3
Download Online
www.sinolingua.com.cn

First Edition 2016

ISBN 978-7-5138-0991-7
Copyright 2016 by Sinolingua Co., Ltd
Published by Sinolingua Co., Ltd
24 Baiwanzhuang Road, Beijing 100037, China
Tel: (86) 10-68320585  68997826
Fax: (86) 10-68997826  68326333
http://www.sinolingua.com.cn
E-mail: hyjx@sinolingua.com.cn
Facebook: www.facebook.com/sinolingua
Printed by Beijing Jinghua Hucais Printing Co., Ltd

*Printed in the People's Republic of China*

# 编者的话

对于广大汉语学习者来说，要想快速提高汉语水平，扩大阅读量是很有必要的。"彩虹桥"汉语分级读物为汉语学习者提供了一系列有趣、有用的汉语阅读材料。本系列读物按照词汇量进行分级，并通过精彩的故事叙述，给读者带来了丰富有趣的阅读享受。本套读物主要有以下特点：

一、**分级精准，循序渐进**。我们参考了新汉语水平考试（HSK）词汇表（2012年修订版）、《汉语国际教育用音节汉字词汇等级划分（国家标准）》和《常用汉语1500高频词语表》等词汇分级标准，结合《欧洲语言教学与评估框架性共同标准》（CEFR），设计了一套适合汉语学习者的"彩虹桥"词汇分级标准。本系列读物分为7个级别（入门级\*、1级、2级、3级、4级、5级、6级），供不同水平的汉语学习者选择，每个级别故事的生词数量不超过本级别对应词汇量的20%。随着级别的升高，故事的篇幅逐渐加长。本系列读物与HSK、CEFR的对应级别，各级词汇量以及每本书的字数详见下表。

---

\* 入门级（Starter）在封底用S标识。

| 级别 | 入门级 | 1级 | 2级 | 3级 | 4级 | 5级 | 6级 |
|---|---|---|---|---|---|---|---|
| 对应级别 | HSK1 CEFR A1 | HSK1-2 CEFR A1-A2 | HSK2-3 CEFR A2-B1 | HSK3 CEFR A2-B1 | HSK3-4 CEFR B1 | HSK4 CEFR B1-B2 | HSK5 CEFR B2-C1 |
| 词汇量 | 150 | 300 | 500 | 750 | 1 000 | 1 500 | 2 500 |
| 字数 | 1 000 | 2 500 | 5 000 | 7 500 | 10 000 | 15 000 | 25 000 |

　　二、**故事精彩，题材多样**。本套读物选材的标准就是"精彩"，所选的故事要么曲折离奇，要么感人至深，对读者构成奇妙的吸引力。选题广泛取材于中国的神话传说、民间故事、文学名著、名人传记和历史故事等，让汉语学习者在阅读中潜移默化地了解中国的文化和历史。

　　三、**结构合理，实用性强**。"彩虹桥"系列读物的每一本书中，除了中文故事正文之外，都配有主要人物的中英文介绍、生词英文注释及例句、故事正文的英文翻译、练习题以及生词表，方便读者阅读和理解故事内容，提升汉语阅读能力。练习题主要采用客观题，题型多样，难度适中，并附有参考答案，既可供汉语教师在课堂上教学使用，又可供汉语学习者进行自我水平检测。

　　如果您对本系列读物有什么想法，比如推荐精彩故事、提出改进意见等，请发邮件到 liuxiaolin@sinolingua.com.cn，与我们交流探讨。也可以关注我们的微信公众号 CHQRainbowBridge，随时与我们交流互动。同时，微信公众号会不定期发布有关"彩虹桥"的出版信息，以及汉语阅读、中国文化小知识等。

韩　颖　刘小琳

# Preface

For students who study Chinese as a foreign language, it's crucial for them to enlarge the scope of their reading to improve their comprehension skills. The "Rainbow Bridge" Graded Chinese Reader series is designed to provide a collection of interesting and useful Chinese reading materials. This series grades each volume by its vocabulary level and brings the learners into every scene through vivid storytelling. The series has the following features:

**I. A gradual approach by grading the volumes based on vocabulary levels.** We have consulted the New HSK Vocabulary (2012 Revised Edition), the *Graded Chinese Syllables, Characters and Words for the Application of Teaching Chinese to the Speakers of Other Languages (National Standard)* and the 1500 Commonly Used High Frequency Chinese Vocabulary, along with the Common European Framework of Reference for Languages (CEFR) to design the "Rainbow Bridge" vocabulary grading standard. The series is divided into seven levels (Starter*, Level 1, Level 2, Level 3, Level 4, Level 5 and Level 6) for students at different stages in their Chinese education to choose from. For each level, new words are no more than 20% of the vocabulary amount as specified in the corresponding HSK and CEFR levels.

---

\* Represented by "S" on the back cover.

As the levels progress, the passage length will in turn increase. The following table indicates the corresponding "Rainbow Bridge" level, HSK and CEFR levels, the vocabulary amount, and number of characters.

| Level | Starter | 1 | 2 | 3 | 4 | 5 | 6 |
|---|---|---|---|---|---|---|---|
| HSK/ CEFR Level | HSK1 CEFR A1 | HSK1-2 CEFR A1-A2 | HSK2-3 CEFR A2-B1 | HSK3 CEFR A2-B1 | HSK3-4 CEFR B1 | HSK4 CEFR B1-B2 | HSK5 CEFR B2-C1 |
| Vocabulary | 150 | 300 | 500 | 750 | 1000 | 1500 | 2500 |
| Characters | 1000 | 2500 | 5000 | 7500 | 10,000 | 15,000 | 25,000 |

**II. Intriguing stories on various themes.** The series features engaging stories known for their twists and turns as well as deeply touching plots. The readers will find it a joyful experience to read the stories. The topics are selected from Chinese mythology, legends, folklore, literary classics, biographies of renowned people and historical tales. Such widely ranged topics would exert an invisible, yet formative, influence on readers' understanding of Chinese culture and history.

**III. Reasonably structured and easy to use.** For each volume of the "Rainbow Bridge" series, apart from a Chinese story, we also provide an introduction to the main characters in Chinese and English, new words with English explanations and sample sentences, and an English translation of the story, followed by comprehension exercises and a vocabulary list to help users read and understand the story and improve their Chinese reading skills. The exercises are mainly presented as objective questions that take on various forms with moderate difficulty. Moreover, keys to the exercises are also provided. The series can be used by teachers in class or by students for self-study.

If you have any questions, comments or suggestions about the series, please email us at liuxiaolin@sinolingua.com.cn. You can also exchange ideas with us via our WeChat account: CHQRainbowBridge. This account will provide updates on the series along with Chinese reading materials and cultural tips.

Han Ying and Liu Xiaolin

# 主要人物
# Main Characters

女　娲 (Nǚwā)：北方的女神，身体一半是人，一半是蛇。
Nüwa: A goddess in the North who was half human and half snake.

龙　妖 (Lóngyāo)：有三个头，吃了很多人，后来被女娲杀死。
Dragon Demon: A demon with three heads that devoured many people but was killed by Nüwa.

大海龟 (Dà Hǎiguī)：有四条坚硬的腿，帮助女娲支撑天和地。
Giant Turtle: A turtle with four sturdy legs who helped Nüwa support the earth and the heaven.

# 中文故事

## 女娲的故事①

在很多很多年以前②,大地上还没有人。天上只有月亮和太阳,地上只有大海③、高山④、森林⑤。

一个女神⑥在高山上睡觉,她的身体一半是人,

① 故事 (gùshi) n.
story
e.g., 妈妈讲了一个很好玩的故事。

② 以前 (yǐqián) n.
earlier times
e.g., 一个月以前,我还在北京旅游。

③ 大海 (dà hǎi) n.
sea
e.g., 蓝色的大海非常美丽。

④ 高山 (gāo shān) n.
high mountain
e.g., 高山上有一片森林。

⑤ 森林 (sēnlín) n.
forest
e.g., 森林里有很多小动物。

⑥ 女神 (nǚshén) n.
goddess
e.g., 她长得很漂亮,像一个女神。

一半是蛇①。这个女神非常漂亮,她姓"风",名字叫"女娲",是北方②的女神。

不知道过了多少年,女娲醒③了。她慢慢坐起来,看看高山,看看大海,再看看天和地。太阳不说话,月亮不说话,大森林也不说话。

① 蛇 (shé) n. snake
e.g., 我不喜欢蛇。

② 北方 (běifāng) n. the North, the northern part
e.g., 我的家在中国北方的一个小城市。

③ 醒 (xǐng) v. wake up
e.g., 他醒了以后,喝了一杯牛奶。

① 孤单 (gūdān) adj. lonely
e.g., 这个小男孩儿一个人玩，觉得很孤单。

女娲很不快乐，她想："这里只有我一个人，太孤单①了，我不喜欢这样！我想有一些朋友。"可是，这儿只有女娲一个人，去哪儿能找到朋友呢？

女娲觉得有点儿饿了，她走进大森林，吃了一点儿水果。森林旁边有水，女娲看到水里有一个

"人"。她想,"好啊!这就是我的朋友吧?"

可是,这个"朋友"不说话,女娲站起来,"她"就站起来;女娲坐下去,"她"就坐下去;女娲跳舞,"她"也跳舞。

① 落 (luò) *v.* fall, drop
e.g., 一只小鸟落在树上，不停地歌唱。

② 影子 (yǐngzi) *n.* reflection, shadow
e.g., 这个孩子就像影子一样跟着我。

"你是谁？你叫什么名字啊？"女娲问。可是"她"不说话，不回答。

这时候，天上开始下雨了，雨水落①在水里，"朋友"就"没有"了！女娲明白了：这个水里的"朋友"就是她的影子②啊！

"把影子当朋友,女娲呀女娲,你真有意思!"她笑了。

"我的影子……我的朋友……"女娲想着想着,就有了个好办法①。她坐下来,看着水里的影子,拿起一块泥土②,和水一起捏③出了一个泥人儿。这个泥人儿眼睛大大的,很漂亮,女娲很喜欢。她把泥人儿

① 办法 (bànfǎ) n. method, idea
e.g., 我突然想到了一个好办法。

② 泥土 (nítǔ) n. mud, earth
e.g., 老人的鞋子上还带着一些泥土。

③ 捏 (niē) v. knead
e.g., 他用泥土捏了一只小兔子。

① 变 (biàn) *v.* become, change
e.g., 几年以后，这里变成了一个现代化的城市。

放在地上，泥人儿就活动起来，成了一个真正的人。

"女娲！女娲！妈妈！妈妈！"这个漂亮的人快乐地唱着、跳着，<u>女娲非常</u>高兴，就拿起泥土，捏出了一个、两个、三个泥人儿……他们都变①成了真正的人，能说话、跳舞、唱歌。他们在<u>女娲</u>的前面，一个拉着一个地唱起歌来：

"天和地最大,女娲是妈妈。

一点儿水,一点儿泥,女娲捏出我和你。"

女娲快乐地捏着泥人儿。饿了,她就吃点东西;渴①了,她就喝雨水;累了,她就睡一会儿。可是,天地太大了,她捏出的泥人儿放在大地上,一会儿就看不见了。

不知道过了多少天,女娲觉得太累了。"这样捏太累了,什么时候才能捏完呢?"她想,"我要想个好办法,快快地做出很多人来。"

女娲看到旁边有一棵②非常高的大树③,树上有着长长的紫藤④。女娲说:"紫

① 渴 (kě) *adj.* thirsty
e.g., 我觉得很渴,要去买水喝。

② 棵 (kē) *m.w.* (used for trees)
e.g., 我家的门口有两棵大树。

③ 树 (shù) *n.* tree
e.g., 这棵大树已经有两百年的历史了。

④ 紫藤 (zǐténg) *n.* wisteria
e.g., 紫藤的花很美丽。

① 飞 (fēi) v. fly
e.g., 很多年以前，人们就梦想着飞上天空。

② 手 (shǒu) n. hand
e.g., 老师的手里拿着好几本中文书。

藤啊，请你帮帮我吧！"

紫藤听到女娲说的话，就从树上飞①了下来，落在了女娲的手②里。女娲拿起紫藤向泥土地上打了一下，地上就飞起了很多泥点儿。这些泥点儿再落在地上，就变成了很多个小人儿。

可是，因为这些小人儿是紫藤"打"出来的，不是女娲捏出来的，所以他们不是很漂亮。有的小人儿太高了，有的小人儿又太矮①了；有的太胖②，有的又很瘦③。不过，女娲也很喜欢这些不漂亮的小人儿。用这个办法，女娲又"打"出

① 矮 (ǎi) *adj.* short
e.g., 她长得很可爱，就是有点儿矮。

② 胖 (pàng) *adj.* fat
e.g., 这个孩子吃得很多，所以有点儿胖。

③ 瘦 (shòu) *adj.* thin
e.g., 别减肥了，你已经很瘦了！

了很多很多个小人儿。

这些小人儿有的跑,有的走,有的哭,有的笑,非常的可爱。女娲觉得,现在这样太有意思了!她站在小人儿的中间,高兴地唱起来:

"太阳和月亮,大海和高山。

女娲一个人,日子太孤单。

一点儿水,一点儿泥,长长紫藤在手里。

有了他,有了你,有了新的天和地!"

小人儿们在大地上快乐地生活,他们有男人、有女人,男人爱上女人,就会结婚、有孩子,生出更多的人。

① 动 (dòng) v. move
e.g., 这只小狗睡醒了，动了一下。

② 支撑 (zhīchēng) v. support
e.g., 她用手臂支撑着身体，跳过了木马。

③ 柱子 (zhùzi) n. pillar
e.g., 这个大房间里有四个巨大的柱子。

④ 断 (duàn) v. break
e.g., 她正在写作业，笔尖突然断了。

⑤ 洞 (dòng) n. hole
e.g., 这座山上有一个山洞。

⑥ 淹没 (yānmò) v. inundate, flood
e.g., 大水淹没了许多人的家。

女娲觉得有点儿累，很想休息休息。可是，有一天，太阳、月亮都看不见了，天向下动①，大地向上动。支撑②天的四个高高的大柱子③，这时候都断④了，倒在地上。很快，天上出现了一个大洞⑤。雨、雪、风一起落下，大水淹没⑥了土地和人们的家。大

水中间还出现了一只龙妖，它吃了很多人。人们不知道应该怎么办，就一起向女娲跑过去，哭着请她帮助。"女娲妈妈，女娲妈妈！天和地怎么了？我们怎么办啊？"

女娲希望人们能快乐、幸福地生活，希望他们每天都能唱歌、跳舞。她努力地

① 补 (bǔ) v. patch
e.g., 妈妈把衣服上的洞补好了。

想办法,"我要怎么做,才能帮助我的孩子们呢?"她不吃也不喝,一天过去了,她想出了办法!

女娲告诉人们:"你们不要哭,我来帮你们把天上的大洞补①好,把龙妖杀死,再给天和地补上四个新的柱子。我要让你们幸福地生活!"

女娲飞到大水上边,

看见龙妖正在水里睡觉。她拿出长长的紫藤，飞到龙妖的头上，这时紫藤变成了一把①宝剑②，女娲用这把宝剑砍③下了龙妖的头。

可是，龙妖又长④出了一个头，它向女娲飞过来，要吃她。女娲向旁边一跳，又砍下了龙妖的第二个头。

① 把 (bǎ) *m.w.* (for sth. in a bunch or with a handle)
e.g., 我送给他一把宝剑作为礼物。

② 宝剑 (bǎojiàn) *n.* sword
e.g., 这把宝剑非常锋利。

③ 砍 (kǎn) *v.* cut
e.g., 他用宝剑砍断了绳子。

④ 长 (zhǎng) *v.* grow
e.g., 十年以后，他长大了，成了一个强壮的小伙子。

① 退 (tuì) *v.* recede
e.g., 大水退去之后,留下了一片泥泞。

② 条 (tiáo) *m.w.* (for sth. long, narrow or thin)
e.g., 这里有一条大河,景色很好。

③ 腿 (tuǐ) *n.* leg
e.g., 他的腿很长,跑得很快。

④ 坚硬 (jiānyìng) *adj.* hard, sturdy
e.g., 大理石的地面非常坚硬。

就这样,女娲和龙妖打了三次,成功地杀死了龙妖。

龙妖死后,大水就退①去了,龙妖吃下去的那些人都从它的身体里跑了出来,回到了家里。

女娲又飞到了东边的大海,那里有一只大海龟。它的四条②腿③长长的,非常坚硬④。

女娲对大海龟说:"大海龟,大海龟,支撑天的四个柱子都断了,人们没

办法生活。我想请你帮助我,借你的四条腿去支撑天和地。"

大海龟觉得女娲做得很对,就点了点头。它把腿借给了女娲,又长出了四条新的腿。

有了大海龟的帮助,女娲重新把天和地支撑起来。可是,天上还有一个

① 石头 (shítou) *n.*
stone
e.g., 我在河边发现了几块好看的小石头。

② 蓝色 (lánsè) *n.*
blue
e.g., 蓝色的天空中有几片白云，天气很好。

③ 黄色 (huángsè) *n.*
yellow
e.g., 我喜欢那件黄色的衣服。

大洞，大洞里还在下着雨、雪，这怎么办呢？

北方的大山很高很高，山上有很多大石头①。这些石头有五个颜色——蓝色②、白色、红色、黑色和黄色③。石头的样子都很漂亮，也很坚硬。

女娲觉得这些石头很好,可以把天上的大洞补上。她对大山说:"大山,大山,天上有一个大洞,我的孩子们不能幸福地生活。我想请你帮助我,借你的石头去补天。"

大山觉得女娲做得很对,就点了点头。大山对石头们说:"去吧,去吧,

① 烧 (shāo) *v.* burn
e.g., 他烧掉了那些信件和照片。
② 熔化 (rónghuà) *v.* melt
e.g., 天气太热了,地面好像都要熔化了!

帮助女娲补天去。"说完,石头们就一块一块地飞了出去。女娲把这些大石头放在一起,用火烧①它们。

很多天以后,石头都熔化②了,女娲就把它们补到天上的大洞里。大洞一点儿一点儿地变小了,雨、雪也一点儿一点儿地变少。

了。到了后来，大洞补好了，天和地跟原来一样了！

太阳出来了，阳光照①在大地上。人们在大地上跳舞，一个孩子唱起歌来：

"天向下，地向上，

① 照 (zhào) *v.* shine
e.g., 阳光照进来，房间里变得明亮了。

① 勇敢 (yǒnggǎn) *adj.* brave, courageous
e.g., 这个小男孩非常勇敢地救出了自己的朋友。

我们怎么办?
谁能去补天?
女娲妈妈好勇敢①,
补好洞,撑起天,
快乐生活到永远!"
　女娲听到他们唱歌,觉得很高兴。她想:"这一次,我真的要好好休息休息了,我太累了!"
　女娲幸福地睡着了,

她长长的头发①变成了大地上的花草,她的身体变成了大地的一部分②。人们想起女娲的时候,就会看看天、看看大地,觉得女娲一直③和他们在一起。

① 头发 (tóufa) *n.*
hair
e.g., 她的头发又黑又长,很美丽。

② 部分 (bùfen) *n.*
part
e.g., 有一部分同学先走了,还有一部分人过一会才走。

③ 一直 (yìzhí) *adv.*
always
e.g., 我一直很喜欢她,可是没有对她说过。

**English Version**

## Nüwa, the Goddess of Mankind

Long before the human race appeared on the earth, there were only oceans, mountains and forests on the earth and the sun and the moon in the sky.

In a great mountain slept a goddess who was half human and half snake. She was a beautiful goddess in the North, whose name was Nüwa and had the family name Feng (Wind).

After sleeping for ages, Nüwa woke up. She sat up slowly and looked at the mountain, the ocean, the sky and the earth. The sun didn't speak, nor did the moon and the forest.

Nüwa felt unhappy. "I'm the only person here," she thought. "I don't want to be so lonely! I really want to have some friends." However, where could she find a friend for there was none except her?

Nüwa felt a little hungry. She entered a big forest, and found some fruits to eat. Along the forest there was a river, in which Nüwa spotted a "person". It occurred to her that this person might become her friend.

However, this friend said nothing. When Nüwa stood up, so did she. When Nüwa sat down, so did she. When Nüwa danced, so did she.

"Who are you? What is your name?" asked Nüwa, but the friend didn't answer.

At that moment, it began to rain. As the rainwater dropped into the river, her friend vanished. Later Nüwa realized "her friend" in the river was none other than her own reflection.

"Oh, Nüwa, it is so funny to mistake your own reflection for your friend," she said as she smiled.

"My reflection… my friend…" After thinking for a while, she came up with a good idea. She sat down and looked at the reflection in the river. She got some soil and molded a figure by mixing it with water. This figure looked pretty with wide eyes, and Nüwa liked it very much. As soon as she put it on the ground, it became a real person and started to move.

"Nüwa! Nüwa! Mama! Mama!" Nüwa was very pleased to see this pretty figure sing and dance with joy; therefore, she got more soil to mold more figures, all of which became real people. They were capable of speaking, dancing and singing. Now, they held each other's hands and began to sing:

"Between the vast heaven and earth,

lives Nüwa our mom.

with a little water, a little mud,

Nüwa molded all of us."

Nüwa kneaded figures blissfully. When hungry, she would find something to eat. When thirsty, she would drink rainwater. When tired, she would take a nap. But the heaven and the earth are so large that the figures she kneaded disappeared as soon as she laid them on the ground.

Day after day, Nüwa finally felt exhausted. "When will I finish the task if I continue in this way?" she thought. "I need to come up with a good solution to make a large number of figures quickly."

Nüwa stood beside a tall tree, in which a long wisteria grew. Nüwa asked, "Wisteria, can you help me?"

Hearing what Nüwa said, the wisteria flew to Nüwa's hand from the tree. Nüwa struck the wisteria towards the earth, from which drops of mud splashed. As these mud drops fell to the ground, they became small figures.

However, these figures were struck by the wisteria rather than kneaded by Nüwa, so they were not beautiful. Some were too tall while the others were too short; some were too big while the others were too small. Even so, Nüwa was fond of these figures anyway. In this manner, Nüwa made a lot of figures.

These figures were so cute. Some ran while others walked; some cried while others smiled. Nüwa thought this was interesting. She stood among these figures and sang happily:

"The sun and the moon, the ocean and high mountains,

I felt so lonely for I was alone.

A little water, and mud, and a long wisteria at hand,

A new world full of people appears on this land."

The figures including men and women lived joyfully on the land. If a man fell in love with a woman, they would marry and have children so the number of people increased.

Nüwa felt a bit tired, so she wanted to take a rest. But one day, the sun and the moon disappeared and the sky moved downward and the ground moved upward. The four high pillars that supported the sky were broken and fell on the ground and a big hole emerged in the sky. Rain and snow all came together and the land and houses were flooded. In the midst of the flood appeared a black Dragon Demon, which devoured many people. Not knowing how to cope with it, the people ran to Nüwa and cried for help. "Nüwa, our mom! What happened to the heaven and the earth? What shall we do?"

Nüwa hoped that the people could live a happy life, singing and dancing every day. She tried her best to find a solution. "What should I do to help my children?" She didn't eat nor drink anything for a whole day, and finally came up with an idea.

Nüwa said to them, "Don't cry. I will help you patch the big hole in the sky. I'll kill the Dragon Demon and replace the four pillars to support the earth and the heaven. I will help you live a happy life!"

Nüwa flew to the surface of the river where she saw the Dragon Demon sleeping in the water. As she flew towards the Dragon Demon with the wisteria, it was transformed into a sword with which Nüwa cut the demon's head off.

However, another head appeared on the Dragon Demon, who flew to Nüwa and wanted to devour her. Nüwa jumped aside, cutting the second head of the demon off. Nüwa fought with the Dragon Demon in this way three times, killing it at last.

After the death of the demon, the big flood receded and the devoured people ran out of the demon's body and returned to their homes.

Nüwa then flew east to the ocean, where there was a giant turtle with four long, sturdy legs.

Nüwa said to the turtle, "Giant Turtle, Giant Turtle, the four pillars supporting the heaven were broken, so my people cannot live. Could you do me a favor and lend your four legs to support the heaven and the earth?"

The Giant Turtle agreed with Nüwa and nodded his head. After lending his legs to Nüwa, the turtle had four new legs.

Thanks to the help of the Giant Turtle, the heaven and the earth were supported again, but there was still a big hole in the sky, through which rain and snow came. What should she do?

The mountains in the North were huge with big stones all over. There were five colors for the stones: blue, white, red, black and yellow. These stones were beautiful and hard.

Nüwa thought these stones were suitable for patching the hole in the sky, so she said to the Mountain, "Your mighty Mountain, due to a big hole in the sky, my children cannot live a happy life. Can you lend me your stones to patch the sky?"

The Mountain nodded his head to show his approval of what Nüwa did. The Mountain said to the stones, "Hurry! Go and help Nüwa patch the sky." After hearing these words, the stones flew away one by one. Nüwa piled the stones together to melt them by fire.

Many days later, the stones were melted and Nüwa mended the big hole with it. As the hole became smaller and smaller, less and less rain and snow came forth. After the big hole was patched, the heaven and the earth became the same as before.

As the sun came out, sunshine began to radiate across the land. Among the people who were dancing, a child began to sing:

"The heaven went down and the earth went up,

What should we do?

Who could patch the sky?

How brave our Mother Nüwa was,

Who had the sky supported and patched,

So we'll live a happy life forever."

Nüwa felt very happy when hearing the song. She thought, "I really need a good rest this time because I am too tired!"

Nüwa fell asleep happily. Her long hair was turned into flowers and grass on the ground, while her body became part of the earth. Today, people will look up at the sky and across the land, and believe that Nüwa is still with them.

# 练习题 Reading exercises

## 一、选择题。Choose the correct answer

1. 女娲姓什么？（　　）

   A. 女　　　B. 娲　　　C. 风　　　D. 伏

2. 女娲走进大森林，吃了什么？（　　）

   A. 雨水　　B. 泥土　　C. 水果　　D. 紫藤

3. 女娲把什么当成了她的朋友？（　　）

   A. 雨水　　B. 另一个人　C. 大树　　D. 她的影子

4. 女娲捏出了多少个泥人儿？（　　）

   A. 一个　　B. 两个　　C. 三个　　D. 很多很多

5. 女娲用什么打出了很多的泥人儿？（　　）

   A. 大树　　　　　　B. 泥土和大树

   C. 紫藤　　　　　　D. 紫藤和大树

6. 有了人做朋友，女娲觉得（　　）。

   A. 很高兴　　　　　B. 有点儿累

   C. 很不快乐　　　　D. 有点儿冷

7. 有一天，支撑天地的大柱子突然断了（　　）。

   A. 一个　　B. 两个　　C. 三个　　D. 四个

8. 吃人的龙妖有几条？（　　）

　　A. 一条　　　B. 两条　　　C. 三条　　　D. 四条

9. 大海龟把几条腿借给了女娲？（　　）

　　A. 一条　　　B. 两条　　　C. 三条　　　D. 四条

10. 女娲补天的大石头一共有几种颜色？（　　）

　　A. 三　　　　B. 五　　　　C. 七　　　　D. 九

二、判断题：请根据故事内容判断下列说法是否正确，如果正确请标"T"，不正确请标"F"。
Decide whether the following statements are true (T) or false (F).

1. 女娲看到天和地之间只有她一个人，觉得很孤单。（　　）
2. 水中的"人"是女娲的影子，所以"她"不说话。（　　）
3. 女娲是照着她的朋友的样子捏泥人儿的。（　　）
4. 女娲捏出的泥人儿，长得都不太好看。（　　）
5. 女娲为了帮助人类要去杀死龙妖，她的武器是一棵大树。（　　）
6. 北边的大海里有一只大海龟，它有四条坚硬的腿。（　　）
7. 补天的石头要先用火来烧，然后才能放到天上去。（　　）
8. 女娲还没有补好天，就永远地睡着了。（　　）
9. 女娲睡着以后，她的长发变成了花草，身体变成了大地的一部分。（　　）

10. 人们非常感谢和喜爱女娲。　　　　　　　（　　）

## 三、选择填空。 Choose the appropriate words to fill in the parentheses.

1. 很多年以前，天和地之间还没有（　　）。天上只有月亮和（　　），地上只有大海、高山、森林。一个名字叫女娲的（　　）在高山上睡觉，她的身体一半是人，一半是（　　）。她有长长的（　　），非常漂亮。醒来以后，她觉得很不快乐，因为天和地之间只有她一个人，她没有（　　）。

　　A. 蛇　　　B. 女神　　C. 人　　　D. 太阳
　　E. 头发　　F. 朋友

2. 女娲（　　）地捏着泥人儿。（　　）了，她就吃点东西；（　　）了，她就喝雨水；（　　）了，她就睡一会儿。可是，天地太（　　）了，她捏出的泥人儿放在大地上，一会儿就看不见了。

　　A. 渴　　　B. 大　　　C. 饿　　　D. 快乐
　　E. 累

3. 有一天,（　　）天空的四个大柱子都断了,（　　）在地上。天空中（　　）了一个大洞。雨、雪、风一起从大洞中冲出,大水（　　）了土地和人类的房子。大水中出现了一条凶恶的龙妖,它吃掉了很多人。人们害怕极了,就一起向女娲（　　）过去,请她帮助。女娲希望人们能快乐地生活,她要（　　）一个办法!

A. 想　　　B. 倒　　　C. 跑　　　D. 淹没

E. 支撑　　F. 出现

## 四、连线题。 Match.

1. 请为下列词语选择合适的搭配。

A. 补好　　　　　　a. 泥人儿

B. 砍下　　　　　　b. 龙妖

C. 淹没　　　　　　c. 龙妖的头

D. 捏出　　　　　　d. 大洞

E. 杀死　　　　　　e. 土地

2. 根据故事内容为下列事物选择各自的特征。

A. 女娲　　　　　a. 长长的

B. 紫藤　　　　　b. 凶恶的

C. 宝剑　　　　　c. 锋利的

D. 龙妖　　　　　d. 美丽的

E. 衣服　　　　　e. 勇敢的

## 五、请根据故事内容给下列句子排列顺序。
## Put the following statements in order according to the story.

A. 人们觉得害怕极了，就一起向女娲跑过去，请她帮助。

B. 女娲用紫藤打出了很多个小人儿，小人儿们在大地上快乐地生活。

C. 女娲和龙妖打了三次，最后终于杀死了龙妖。

D. 龙妖死后，大水就不见了，龙妖吃下去的那些人都得救了。

E. 突然有一天，天空中出现了一个大洞，雨、雪、风从洞中冲出。

F. 大水淹没了土地和人类的房子。大水中出现了一条凶恶的龙妖，它吃了很多人。

## 六、图片题。 Answer the following questions according to the picture.

1. 请根据图片说说这幅图应该放在这本书的第（　　）页。

2. 图片中都有什么人物？

3. 图中的人物在做什么？

4. 他们的心情怎么样？

5. 请你用中文或英文给这幅图加一个简单的标题说明。

**练习题答案 Keys to the exercises**

一、选择题
1. C  2. C  3. D  4. D  5. C
6. A  7. D  8. A  9. D  10. B

二、判断题：请根据故事内容判断下列说法是否正确，如果正确请标"T"，不正确请标"F"
1. T  2. T  3. F  4. F  5. F
6. F  7. T  8. F  9. T  10. T

三、选择填空
1. C    D    B    A    E    F
2. D    C    A    E    B
3. E    B    F    D    C    A

四、连线题
1. A-d, B-c, C-e, D-a, E-b    2. A-e, B-a, C-c, D-b, E-d

五、请根据故事内容给下列句子排列顺序
B-E-F-A-C-D

# 词汇表
## Vocabulary List

| | | | |
|---|---|---|---|
| 矮 | *adj.* | ǎi | short |
| 把 | *m.w.* | bǎ | (for sth. in a bunch or with a handle) |
| 办法 | *n.* | bànfǎ | method, approach |
| 宝剑 | *n.* | bǎojiàn | sword |
| 北方 | *n.* | běifāng | the North, the northern part |
| 变 | *v.* | biàn | become, change |
| 补 | *v.* | bǔ | patch |
| 部分 | *n.* | bùfen | part |
| 长 | *v.* | zhǎng | grow |
| 大海 | *n.* | dà hǎi | sea |
| 动 | *v.* | dòng | move |
| 洞 | *n.* | dòng | hole |
| 断 | *v.* | duàn | break |
| 飞 | *v.* | fēi | fly |
| 高山 | *n.* | gāo shān | high mountain |
| 孤单 | *adj.* | gūdān | lonely |
| 故事 | *n.* | gùshi | story |
| 黄色 | *n.* | huángsè | yellow |
| 坚硬 | *adj.* | jiānyìng | hard, sturdy |
| 砍 | *v.* | kǎn | cut |
| 棵 | *m.w.* | kē | (used for trees) |
| 渴 | *adj.* | kě | thirsty |
| 蓝色 | *n.* | lánsè | blue |
| 落 | *v.* | luò | fall, drop |
| 泥土 | *n.* | nítǔ | mud, earth |
| 捏 | *v.* | niē | knead |
| 女神 | *n.* | nǚshén | goddess |
| 胖 | *adj.* | pàng | fat |
| 熔化 | *v.* | rónghuà | melt |

| | | | |
|---|---|---|---|
| 森林 | n. | sēnlín | forest |
| 烧 | v. | shāo | burn |
| 蛇 | n. | shé | snake |
| 石头 | n. | shítou | stone |
| 手 | n. | shǒu | hand |
| 瘦 | adj. | shòu | thin |
| 树 | n. | shù | tree |
| 条 | m.w. | tiáo | (for sth. long, narrow or thin) |
| 头发 | n. | tóufa | hair |
| 腿 | n. | tuǐ | leg |
| 退 | v. | tuì | recede |
| 醒 | v. | xǐng | wake up |
| 淹没 | v. | yānmò | inundate, flood |
| 一直 | adv. | yìzhí | always |
| 以前 | n. | yǐqián | earlier times |
| 影子 | n. | yǐngzi | reflection, shadow |
| 勇敢 | adj. | yǒnggǎn | brave, courageous |
| 照 | v. | zhào | shine |
| 支撑 | v. | zhīchēng | support |
| 柱子 | n. | zhùzi | pillar |
| 紫藤 | n. | zǐténg | wisteria |

项目策划：刘小琳　韩　颖
责任编辑：刘小琳
英文编辑：韩芙芸
英文翻译：吴爱俊
封面设计：E·T创意工作室

**图书在版编目（CIP）数据**

女娲的故事：汉、英 / 韩颖改编．— 北京：华语教学出版社，2016
（"彩虹桥"汉语分级读物．一级：300词）
ISBN 978-7-5138-0991-7

Ⅰ．①女… Ⅱ．①韩… Ⅲ．①汉语－对外汉语教学－语言读物 Ⅳ．① H195.5

中国版本图书馆 CIP 数据核字（2015）第 155711 号

### 女娲的故事
韩　颖　改编

＊

©华语教学出版社有限责任公司
华语教学出版社有限责任公司出版
（中国北京百万庄大街24号　邮政编码 100037）
电话：(86)10-68320585　68997826
传真：(86)10-68997826　68326333
网址：www.sinolingua.com.cn
电子信箱：hyjx@sinolingua.com.cn
新浪微博地址：http://weibo.com/sinolinguavip
北京京华虎彩印刷有限公司印刷
2016年（32开）第1版
2016年第1版第1次印刷
（汉英）
ISBN 978-7-5138-0991-7
定价：15.00元